Tit                                                    eep
R.
PT          D0970302
TS

# Dear Parent:
## Your child's love of reading starts here!

Every child learns to read in a different way and at his or her own speed. Some go back and forth between reading levels and read favorite books again and again. Others read through each level in order. You can help your young reader improve and become more confident by encouraging his or her own interests and abilities. From books your child reads with you to the first books he or she reads alone, there are I Can Read Books for every stage of reading:

### SHARED READING
Basic language, word repetition, and whimsical illustrations, ideal for sharing with your emergent reader

### BEGINNING READING
Short sentences, familiar words, and simple concepts for children eager to read on their own

### READING WITH HELP
Engaging stories, longer sentences, and language play for developing readers

### READING ALONE
Complex plots, challenging vocabulary, and high-interest topics for the independent reader

### ADVANCED READING
Short paragraphs, chapters, and exciting themes for the perfect bridge to chapter books

I Can Read Books have introduced children to the joy of reading since 1957. Featuring award-winning authors and illustrators and a fabulous cast of beloved characters, I Can Read Books set the standard for beginning readers.

A lifetime of discovery begins with the magical words "I Can Read!"

*Visit www.icanread.com for information*
*on enriching your child's reading experience.*

*For Shawn and
Phil, up at the
top of our Barton
cousin pyramid
—C.B.*

*To Doug.
Let's go ride bikes!
—T.C.*

Clarence was just a muddy pickup.

One day, there was a big storm.

Lightning zapped the car wash.

Now Clarence has a secret.

Water turns him into Mighty Truck!

I Can Read Book® is a trademark of HarperCollins Publishers.

Mighty Truck: Zip and Beep Copyright © 2018 by HarperCollins Publishers. All rights reserved. Manufactured in China. No part of this book may be used or reproduced in any manner whatsoever without written permission except in the case of brief quotations embodied in critical articles and reviews. For information address HarperCollins Children's Books, a division of HarperCollins Publishers, 195 Broadway, New York, NY 10007.
www.icanread.com

Library of Congress Control Number: 2017962821
ISBN 978-0-06-234473-1 (trade bdg.) — ISBN 978-0-06-234472-4 (pbk.)

18  19  20  21  22   SCP   10  9  8  7  6  5  4  3  2  1   ❖   First Edition

# I Can Read!

BEGINNING
**1**
READING

# MIGHTY TRUCK

## ZIP AND BEEP

BY *CHRIS BARTON*  ILLUSTRATED BY *TROY CUMMINGS*

Jackson County Public Library
Seymour, Indiana 47274

WITHDRAWN

**HARPER**
*An Imprint of HarperCollinsPublishers*

Clarence had been one busy truck.

No, make that two busy trucks.

"I need a day off," Clarence said.

He hoped his boss would understand.

And she did.

"I know how you feel," Hattie said.

"I need a day off, too."

Hattie's cousins were visiting.

She needed to spend time with them.

"I have an idea," Clarence said.

"I can show your cousins around.

That can be my day off."

"It's a deal," Hattie agreed.

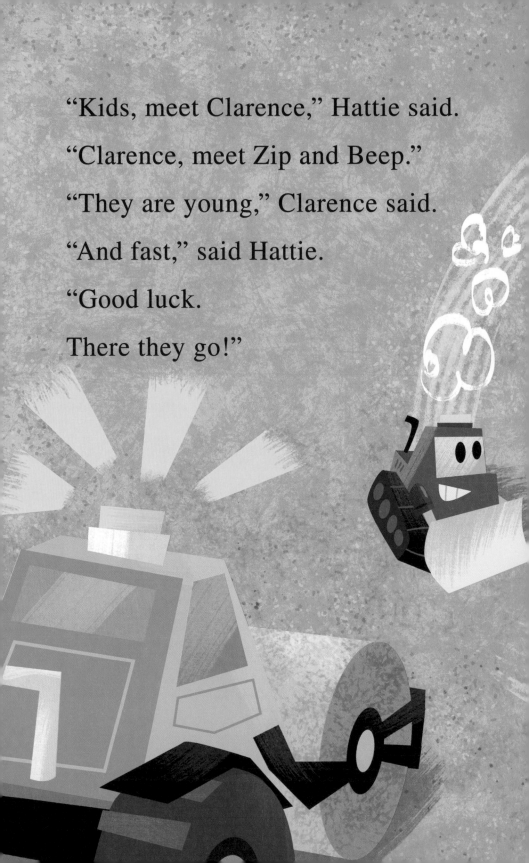

"Kids, meet Clarence," Hattie said.

"Clarence, meet Zip and Beep."

"They are young," Clarence said.

"And fast," said Hattie.

"Good luck.

There they go!"

Clarence chased Zip and Beep.

He chased them before lunch.

Clarence chased them during lunch.

He chased them after lunch.

He pretty much skipped lunch.

The day was only half done.

Zip and Beep had energy to burn.

Not Clarence.

He was burned out.

But Clarence knew a way to cool down.

He just had to make it to the park.

Clarence used to play at the park.

Hide-and-seek was his favorite.

"I will count," Clarence said.

Zip and Beep zoomed and hid.

Clarence counted to seventy-nine.

"Ready or not, here I come!"

It was time to find Zip and Beep.

It was time for something else, too.

Time for the park's sprinklers.

Clarence got soaking wet.

That changed him into Mighty Truck.

"All right!" Mighty Truck said.

"Let's go!

I'll show Zip and Beep

every game I know!"

17

Mighty Truck found Zip and Beep.

He found them fast.

"Really fast," said Zip.

"Really, wheely fast," added Beep.

"Where is Clarence?" they asked.

"He must be hiding," Mighty Truck said.

"Who's up for tag?"

After tag, everyone played freeze tag.

After that, they played shadow tag.

"Now what?" Zip asked.

Mighty Truck suggested jump rope.

"We don't have a rope," Beep said.

"No problem," said Mighty Truck.

They jumped with jumper cables.

Next everyone played kick the can.

Then they played red light, green light.

Then everyone played leapfrog.

Then they played
"Mighty Truck, may I?"

Mighty Truck was out of ideas.

Zip and Beep were out of energy.

So they all played in the sand.

"Can we bury you?" Zip yawned.

"Please, Mighty Truck?" Beep yawned.

"Start digging," Mighty Truck said.

Hattie found them in the sandbox.

The young bulldozers were sleeping.

Clarence was dozing, too.

He was also a sandy mess.

"You fell asleep!" Hattie teased.

"You were supposed to watch them."

"I did watch them," Clarence said.

"I watched them cover me with sand."

Hattie chuckled.

"Thanks for your help," she said.

"You did a mighty good job."

"If you only knew," Clarence said.

"I need a real day off tomorrow."

"Great!" Hattie replied.

"I'll have more cousins visiting."

"Never mind," Clarence said.

"Days off are too much work."

DEC 05 2014

DEC 0 5 2018